PROMISES
FOR THE
OVERCOMER

8 ESSENTIAL GUARANTEES
FOR SPIRITUAL VICTORY

DR. DAVID JEREMIAH

W Publishing Group

An Imprint of Thomas Nelson

Published in Nashville, Tennessee, by W Publishing, an imprint of Thomas Nelson.

Published in association with Yates & Yates, www.yates2.com.

Thomas Nelson titles may be purchased in bulk for educational, business, fund-raising, or sales promotional use. For information, please e-mail SpecialMarkets@ThomasNelson.com.

Unless otherwise noted, Scripture quotations are taken from the New King James Version®. © 1982 by Thomas Nelson. Used by permission. All rights reserved.

Scripture quotations marked NIV are from the Holy Bible, New International Version®, NIV®. Copyright © 1973, 1978, 1984, 2011 by Biblica, Inc.® Used by permission of Zondervan. All rights reserved worldwide. www.Zondervan.com. The "NIV" and "New International Version" are trademarks registered in the United States Patent and Trademark Office by Biblica, Inc.®

Any Internet addresses, phone numbers, or company or product information printed in this book are offered as a resource and are not intended in any way to be or to imply an endorsement by Thomas Nelson, nor does Thomas Nelson vouch for the existence, content, or services of these sites, phone numbers, companies, or products beyond the life of this book.

Library of Congress Control Number: 2018908730

ISBN 978-0-7852-2628-4

Printed in the United States of America

20 21 22   LSC   10 9 8 7 6 5 4 3

CONTENTS

Introduction   v

Chapter 1: We Are Promised Strength   1
Chapter 2: We Are Promised Truth   7
Chapter 3: We Are Promised Goodness   13
Chapter 4: We Are Promised Peace   19
Chapter 5: We Are Promised Faith   26
Chapter 6: We Are Promised Wisdom   32
Chapter 7: We Are Promised Victory Over
            Temptation   38
Chapter 8: We Are Promised Answers to
            Our Prayers   44

Notes   51

INTRODUCTION

It was one of the most inspirational rallying cries in history. Prior to the Allied forces' invasion of Normandy, also known as D-Day, General Dwight D. Eisenhower sent the following message to his troops:

> Soldiers, Sailors, and Airmen of the Allied Expeditionary Force!
>
> You are about to embark upon the Great Crusade, toward which we have striven these many months. The eyes of the world are upon you. The hopes and prayers of liberty-loving people everywhere march with you. In company with our brave Allies and brothers-in-arms on other Fronts, you will bring about the destruction of the German war machine, the elimination of Nazi tyranny over the oppressed peoples of Europe, and security for ourselves in a free world.
>
> Your task will not be an easy one. Your enemy is well trained, well equipped, and battle hardened. He will fight savagely. . . .

> I have full confidence in your devotion to duty and skill in battle.
>
> We will accept nothing less than full Victory!
>
> Good Luck! And let us all beseech the blessing of Almighty God upon this great and noble undertaking.[1]

Of course, with the benefit of hindsight and history, we know General Eisenhower's confidence in both the operation and his troops was well deserved. The invasion of Normandy was a strategic success that turned the tide of World War II and foreshadowed the "full Victory" Eisenhower described.

But what if the invasion had not gone well? What if the Allies had encountered defeat instead of victory? That was a scenario General Eisenhower considered in great detail. In fact, on the evening before D-Day, he wrote a brief note accepting responsibility for the operation's failure should the day be lost:

> Our landings in the Cherbourg-Havre area have failed to gain a satisfactory foothold and I have withdrawn the troops. My decision to attack at this time and place was based upon the best

information available. The troops, the air, and the Navy did all that bravery and devotion to duty could do. If any blame or fault attaches to the attempt, it is mine alone.[2]

As someone who has deeply appreciated the blessing of freedom throughout my life, I'm grateful that message was never sent.

THE BATTLE IS REAL

You may never have commanded an army or faced off against another person in hand-to-hand combat. But if you are a disciple of Jesus Christ, then you have more in common with General Eisenhower than you may realize. For example, you know what it's like to be part of a war—an expansive conflict in which the stakes are incredibly high. And you know what it's like to face an enemy who is "well trained, well equipped, and battle hardened." One that will "fight savagely" at every turn in an effort to destroy you.

I'm talking, of course, about the spiritual battle we face as Christians. According to God's Word, this spiritual battle is currently raging on two fronts.

The first front is cosmic in scale. It's the battle

between good and evil, between God's kingdom and the kingdom of this world. The apostle Paul described this front in his letter to the Christians in Ephesus: "For we do not wrestle against flesh and blood, but against principalities, against powers, against the rulers of the darkness of this age, against spiritual hosts of wickedness in the heavenly places. Therefore take up the whole armor of God, that you may be able to withstand in the evil day, and having done all, to stand" (Eph. 6:12–13).

The second front is more personal. It's the battle between right and wrong in our hearts as individuals—between rebellion against God and obedience to His will. It's the daily struggle to put to death our sinful nature and embrace the righteousness we have received through Christ. Paul described this front in his letter to the Christians at Corinth: "For though we walk in the flesh, we do not war according to the flesh. For the weapons of our warfare are not carnal but mighty in God for pulling down strongholds, casting down arguments and every high thing that exalts itself against the knowledge of God, bringing every thought into captivity to the obedience of Christ, and being ready to punish all disobedience when your obedience is fulfilled" (2 Cor. 10:3–6).

Make no mistake: both phases of this battle are

real, and both affect every single follower of Christ—whether we realize it or not.

THE BATTLE IS ALREADY WON

You don't have to look far to see the ravages and destruction this spiritual battle has caused. Just watch the news. Just listen to your own heart.

On the cosmic front, it's clear that our world is filled with pain. Both today and throughout history, the human race has endured war and terror, poverty and prejudice, disaster and death—the list goes on. Sometimes we can't help but feel like everything is ripping apart at the seams.

On the personal front, so many people in our culture—Christians and non-Christians alike—feel crushed by the weight of anxiety, fear, loneliness, and confusion. We deal with the constant pull of temptation. We are intimately aware of the darkness in our own hearts.

That's the bad news.

The good news, however, is incredible: the battle has already been won. Our enemy was decisively defeated through the death and resurrection of Jesus Christ (Col. 2:14–15). The universe will be made new and made whole once again. As disciples of Jesus, we will live to see the day when the darkness in our hearts is forever extinguished by the light of our Creator.

That is the promise of God's Word:

Now I saw a new heaven and a new earth, for the first heaven and the first earth had passed away. Also there was no more sea. Then I, John, saw the holy city, New Jerusalem, coming down out of heaven from God, prepared as a bride adorned for her husband. And I heard a loud voice from heaven saying, "Behold, the tabernacle of God is with men, and He will dwell with them, and they shall be His people. God Himself will be with them and be their God. And God will wipe away every tear from their eyes; there shall be no more death, nor sorrow, nor crying. There shall be no more pain, for the former things have passed away."

Then He who sat on the throne said, "Behold, I make all things new." And He said to me, "Write, for these words are true and faithful." (Rev. 21:1–5)

This truth is the essential difference between our situation as Christians and that of General Eisenhower on the eve of that landmark battle. As the leader of a human army, Eisenhower had to consider and plan for the possibility of defeat. As servants of Christ, we need only think of victory.

WE ARE OVERCOMERS

If you serve the Lord Jesus Christ, as I do, that means you are a disciple of the One who has "overcome the world" (John 16:33). That makes you an Overcomer.

To be an Overcomer means to live in light of the victory God has already won on our behalf. It means we choose to walk in that victory each day as members of His kingdom. It means we choose to win the fight against fear, speak truth instead of falsehood, promote wisdom rather than confusion, and more.

Are you ready for such a life? For those of us who choose to live as Overcomers, God has promised several key blessings throughout His Word. In this booklet, we will focus on eight of those promised blessings: strength, truth, goodness, peace, faith, wisdom, victory over temptation, and prayer.

These promises will serve as the foundation for your daily life as an Overcomer. Are you ready?

CHAPTER 1

WE ARE PROMISED STRENGTH

In October 2016, a nearly 400-pound behemoth of a man named Ray Williams took the stage at the USA Powerlifting Nationals in Atlanta, Georgia. Visibly bursting with confidence, Williams settled himself under a weight bar holding a total of 1,005 pounds.

What happened next had never happened before.

Williams lifted the bar off the rack, stepped back, and then performed a flawless power squat. Meaning, he squatted down until his thighs were parallel to the ground—if you watch the video, you can see the heavy steel bar actually bending as it lay across Williams's shoulders—and then exploded upward until he returned both himself and the weight bar to a standing position. Then, with the cheers of the crowd ringing around him, Williams placed the bar back on the rack and raised his hands in victory as the first person to successfully "raw squat" more than 1,000 pounds during an official competition.[1]

Obviously, Ray Williams knows a lot about strength. But so do I—not because I have bulging muscles or some elevated athletic prowess, but because I am an Overcomer. I am a servant of Jesus Christ, which means I am empowered by the same Holy Spirit that called galaxies out of nothing and set in place the foundations of the universe.

The same is true of you.

CONTAGIOUS STRENGTH

After liberating His people from generations of bondage in Egypt, God brought the Israelites to the brink of the promised land. These people had seen incredible demonstrations of God's power—the devastation of the ten plagues, the miracle of God parting the Red Sea, the terrifying glimpse of God's presence on Mount Sinai, and more.

Yet despite their recent experiences with God's limitless strength, the Israelites were still prone to fear. They still operated from a perspective of weakness. And nothing demonstrated that weakness better than their rejection of God's blessing in the book of Numbers.

It all started when twelve spies returned from Canaan—the promised land—and reported everything they had seen and encountered. Ten of those spies were frightened out of their wits:

But the men who had gone up with him said, "We are not able to go up against the people, for they are stronger than we." And they gave the children of Israel a bad report of the land which they had spied out, saying, "The land through which we have gone as spies is a land that devours its inhabitants, and all the people whom we saw in it are men of great stature. There we saw the giants (the descendants of Anak came from the giants); and we were like grasshoppers in our own sight, and so we were in their sight." (Num. 13:31–33)

Have you noticed the way weakness and fear can be contagious? That's what happened among God's people. The words of the spies sent shockwaves of terror throughout the community: "And all the children of Israel complained against Moses and Aaron, and the whole congregation said to them, 'If only we had died in the land of Egypt! Or if only we had died in this wilderness! Why has the Lord brought us to this land to fall by the sword, that our wives and children should become victims? Would it not be better for us to return to Egypt?'" (14:2–3).

The tumult and terror of that moment was so deep that even "Moses and Aaron fell on their faces before all the assembly . . . of Israel" (v. 5).

Two men stood apart from the crowd in the midst

of that chaos. They had also traveled throughout the promised land as spies. They had seen the fortifications of the Canaanite cities and the formidable size of the Canaanite warriors. They had every reason to join with everyone else in wishing they could return to the safety and security of their bondage in Egypt.

And yet those two men were not afraid:

> Joshua son of Nun and Caleb son of Jephunneh, who were among those who had explored the land, tore their clothes and said to the entire Israelite assembly, "The land we passed through and explored is exceedingly good. If the Lord is pleased with us, he will lead us into that land, a land flowing with milk and honey, and will give it to us. Only do not rebel against the Lord. And do not be afraid of the people of the land, because we will devour them. Their protection is gone, but the Lord is with us. Do not be afraid of them." (Num. 14:6–9, NIV)

Joshua and Caleb were Overcomers. They were not focused on the obstacles in front of them; they were focused on what God had promised. They were focused on God Himself, and that focus empowered them to overcome weakness with strength.

Notice that Joshua and Caleb took a stand against the weakness in their own community.

That's important. Because it's one thing to be strong when you're fighting an enemy—to buck up and stand your ground when someone is attacking you. But it's something entirely different to speak up and take a stand for God in the face of people you care about.

We need more of that strength within the church.

STRENGTH FOR TODAY

If you're anything like me, you have moments in your life when you feel weak. When you lack strength or conviction. When you're not sure what to do or what to say or how to hold your ground in a world that feels like it's rushing farther and farther away from God's plan each day.

Those moments reveal our weakness as human beings. But that's okay. Because like Caleb and Joshua, we don't have to focus on our weakness. We can focus on what God has promised. And what God has promised is that we can overcome our weakness with His strength:

- "I can do all things through Christ who strengthens me" (Phil. 4:13).
- "But those who wait on the Lord shall renew their strength; they shall mount up with wings like eagles, they shall run and not be weary, they shall walk and not faint" (Isa. 40:31).

- "For God has not given us a spirit of fear, but of power and of love and of a sound mind" (2 Tim. 1:7).

As a disciple of Jesus, you are an Overcomer. That means each of those Scripture passages has direct application for your life. They were written for you, and they are true. You can trust them, and you can experience God's strength even in those moments when you feel weak.

Just as importantly, this call to be empowered by God's strength is not a suggestion. As an Overcomer in God's kingdom, He has commanded you to "be strong in the Lord and in the power of His might" (Eph. 6:10). He has commanded you to "watch, stand fast in the faith, be brave, be strong" (1 Cor. 16:13).

How will you respond?

Heavenly Father,

I am aware that in my own resources, I have no strength. I am weak. Yet I am not afraid—because You are strong.

I declare my belief in Your Word. I proclaim the truth that I can do all things through Christ—because He strengthens me. I accept Your promise to overcome my weakness with Your incalculable strength, and I praise You for all You will accomplish in and through my life.

Thank You, Father, for the gift of strength. Amen.

CHAPTER 2

WE ARE PROMISED TRUTH

For about thirty years, the American Dialect Society has chosen a "Word of the Year" as a way of highlighting how the English language continues to change, and to celebrate specific terms or phrases from recent history. Often, these "Word of the Year" winners reflect key crises or problems from a given year. That was the case with *subprime* in 2007, for example. And with *Y2K* in 1999.

The "Word of the Year" choice for 2017 was particularly disheartening. The winner was *fake news*, which the ADS defined in two ways:

1. "Disinformation or falsehoods presented as real news," and
2. "Actual news that is claimed to be untrue."[1]

What a perfect definition for this phenomenon, which has continued to gain force in recent years. And what a sad reflection on today's culture that we cannot even agree whether the news is true or false.

Thankfully, we as Overcomers don't have to rely on news organizations or politicians to determine what is real or fake. Nor are we bound to our culture's continually shifting definitions of what is right, wrong, or indifferent.

We have access to truth.

THE TRUTH ABOUT TRUTH

People have been searching for truth throughout human history. We typically search for it in the same way we search for gold or diamonds or other natural resources—meaning, we believe truth exists somewhere in the universe, but it's hidden. It's out of reach, and we must move beyond our ordinary circumstances in order to seek it, find it, and take hold of it in our lives.

But that's not the truth about truth. Thank goodness!

One of the most revolutionary principles established in God's Word is that truth is not a thing or concept or an idea. Instead, truth is a Person. Truth is not a what, but a Who.

How do we know that truth is a Person? Because the very first words of the Bible are, "In the beginning God" (Gen. 1:1). That is the ultimate definition of reality. Before there was anything, there was God. Which means God is the source of everything—including truth.

The apostle John elaborated on this reality in the very first paragraph of his Gospel:

> In the beginning was the Word, and the Word was with God, and the Word was God. He was in the beginning with God. All things were made through Him, and without Him nothing was made that was made. In Him was life, and the life was the light of men. And the light shines in the darkness, and the darkness did not comprehend it. (John 1:1–5)

The "Him" John referenced is none other than Jesus Christ—the same Jesus who declared Himself to be "the way, *the truth*, and the life" (John 14:6, emphasis added).

Don't miss the weight of that reality. Jesus has always been with God because Jesus *is* God. They are One. And Jesus knows all things because "all things were made through Him." There is nothing that can be known, understood, or experienced that doesn't have its source in the Lord Jesus. Therefore, Jesus is not only the source of truth: He is truth.

NOT SEEKING, BUT SOUGHT

As Overcomers, we've been promised access to the truth. In fact, we are commanded to "stand therefore, having girded your waist with truth" (Eph. 6:14). We are expected to wrap ourselves with truth in the same way Roman soldiers cinched together the different elements of their armor with a belt.

When we understand that truth is a Person, however, we can let go of the notion that truth must be subjective. Or created. Or earned. We can let go of our modern belief that truth is reserved for the elite—for those with graduate degrees or those who spend their time in some deep contemplation of the universe and all its mysteries.

The apostle John made it clear that Jesus, the Truth, is not hidden or waiting to be found: "And the Word became flesh and dwelt among us, and we beheld His glory, the glory as of the only begotten of the Father, full of grace and truth" (John 1:14).

The good news of the gospel is that Truth discovers us. As Overcomers who live and serve in God's kingdom, we don't just seek after the truth; we are sought *by* the Truth. I like what A. W. Tozer wrote: "Truth is not a thing for which we must search, but a Person to whom we must hearken!"[2]

Of course, one of the ways Jesus pursues us with the truth is through His Word, the Bible.

- "Sanctify them by Your truth. Your word is truth. As You sent Me into the world, I also have sent them into the world. And for their sakes I sanctify Myself, that they also may be sanctified by the truth" (John 17:17–19).
- "All Scripture is given by inspiration of God, and is profitable for doctrine, for reproof, for correction, for instruction in righteousness, that the man of God may be complete, thoroughly equipped for every good work" (2 Tim. 3:16–17).
- "The law of the Lord is perfect, converting the soul; the testimony of the Lord is sure, making wise the simple; the statutes of the Lord are right, rejoicing the heart; the commandment of the Lord is pure, enlightening the eyes; the fear of the Lord is clean, enduring forever; the judgments of the Lord are true and righteous altogether" (Psalm 19:7–9).

You are an Overcomer in God's kingdom, which means you have direct access to the same truth that has defined reality since the beginning of the world and beyond. Will you receive it?

Heavenly Father,

I proclaim my belief that You, and You alone, are truth. You are the source of truth, and You are the standard by which everything else is measured.

I believe the promise in Your Word that I can know You as the truth, and that by knowing the truth I can be set free. I want to be free from my sin and from the deceptive messages of the world around me. I want to build my life on the truth of Your Word.

Thank You, Father, for the gift of truth. Amen.

CHAPTER 3

WE ARE PROMISED GOODNESS

Do you remember Psalm 23? "The Lord is my shepherd; I shall not want. He makes me to lie down in green pastures; He leads me beside the still waters. He restores my soul" (vv. 1–3). For generation after generation, Psalm 23 has remained one of the most popular chapters in the Bible—and with good reason. It's a vivid picture of God's provision, care, and rest.

Yet even a poem as idyllic as Psalm 23 does not gloss over the reality of evil in our world. That reality is present in verse 4: "Yea, though I walk through the valley of the shadow of death, I will fear no evil."

I like what Frederick Buechner has written about that verse:

> The psalm does not pretend that evil and death do not exist. Terrible things happen, and they happen to good people as well as to bad people. Even the paths of righteousness lead through

the valley of the shadow. Death lies ahead for all of us, saints and sinners alike, and for all the ones we love. The psalmist doesn't try to explain evil. He doesn't try to minimize evil. He simply says he will not fear evil. For all the power that evil has, it doesn't have the power to make him afraid.[1]

You already know that evil exists. You already know that evil is dangerous and destructive. What I want to show you now is that you don't have to be afraid. Because as an Overcomer, you've been promised the goodness of God.

GOD IS GOOD

The Bible is filled with declarations and proclamations about the goodness of God. As we saw with truth in the previous chapter, God is both the definition of good and the ultimate source of any goodness in this world or anywhere else.

- "Oh, taste and see that the Lord is good; blessed is the man who trusts in Him!" (Psalm 34:8).
- "Every good gift and every perfect gift is from above, and comes down from the Father of

lights, with whom there is no variation or shadow of turning" (James 1:17).

- "So [Jesus] said to him, 'Why do you call Me good? No one is good but One, that is, God'" (Matt. 19:17).

That final verse may seem discouraging. Jesus was teaching a large crowd when a rich young man approached Him and asked: "Good Teacher, what good thing shall I do that I may have eternal life?" (v. 16). Jesus responded by proclaiming that "no one is good but . . . God."

That begs the question: *If only God is good, does that mean we can never be good? Will we always have to put up with the shadow of evil and sin and death?*

The answer is that we cannot become good in and of ourselves; however, we can receive God's goodness. We can become good because He is good. As the apostle Paul wrote: "For [God] made [Christ] who knew no sin to be sin for us, that we might become the righteousness of God in Him" (2 Cor. 5:21).

When Jesus died on the cross, He took on our identity as a sinner. When we believe in Him, we take on His identity as the righteous Son of God. He gives His righteousness to us—His goodness. We receive it when we believe that Jesus is the Son of God, repent of our sin, and ask for forgiveness.

WE CAN ACCOMPLISH GOOD

As Overcomers, we don't exist in a passive state of goodness. Instead, we have the power to act in ways that reflect the goodness we have received through Christ. Indeed, we are called to "overcome evil with good" (Rom. 12:21).

One of the ways we actively produce good in the world is to obey Jesus' Great Commission:

> And Jesus came and spoke to them, saying, "All authority has been given to Me in heaven and on earth. Go therefore and make disciples of all the nations, baptizing them in the name of the Father and of the Son and of the Holy Spirit, teaching them to observe all things that I have commanded you; and lo, I am with you always, even to the end of the age." Amen. (Matt. 28:18–20)

The message of the gospel is the essence of goodness. It is *the* good news. As Overcomers, we are commanded to proclaim that message to all who will hear. And we are promised not only God's guidance as we seek to obey this command but also His presence. He is with us.

Another way we can actively produce goodness in the world is to develop the fruit of the Spirit in our lives and in our community as the church: "But the fruit of the Spirit is love, joy, peace, longsuffering, kindness, *goodness*, faithfulness, gentleness, self-control. Against such there is no law" (Gal. 5:22–23, emphasis added).

Notice that the fruit of the Spirit is singular. It's "fruit," not "fruits." That means we don't focus on developing peace one day and then faithfulness a week from Tuesday. Rather, as the Holy Spirit transforms our lives, we develop each element of that "fruit"—including goodness. And the more of that fruit we demonstrate to the world, the more we overcome the world's evil with God's good.

Don't ignore the Bible's command for God's people to promote God's goodness in the world:

- "He has shown you, O man, what is good; and what does the Lord require of you but to do justly, to love mercy, and to walk humbly with your God?" (Mic. 6:8).
- "Therefore, as we have opportunity, let us do good to all, especially to those who are of the household of faith" (Gal. 6:10).
- "Who is wise and understanding among you? Let him show by good conduct that his works are done in the meekness of wisdom" (James 3:13).

The end of Psalm 23 is a perfect promise for Overcomers working to achieve good in the world: "Surely goodness and mercy shall follow me all the days of my life; and I will dwell in the house of the Lord forever" (v. 6).

Heavenly Father,

You, and You alone, are good. I cannot demonstrate Your goodness in my own strength. I have no righteousness other than that which You have given me through Christ.

Thank You, heavenly Father, for Your gift of goodness. I receive it, and I desire to be continually changed by it. I commit to reflecting Your goodness in the world each day. I accept Your command to overcome evil with good. Amen.

CHAPTER 4

WE ARE PROMISED PEACE

Take a moment to imagine yourself resting on a boat in the middle of a lake. It's a summer day, and you are laying on your back with your head on a cushion. Your eyes are closed, and you can feel the sunshine warming the skin on your face. You hear the sound of birds singing in the distance. A gentle breeze stirs across the water—you can feel it tickle your arms as the boat begins to lazily rock back and forth.

Would you feel at peace in that moment? If you kept your eyes closed for just a few more minutes, would you drift off to sleep with the gentle rocking of the current?

Most people would say "Yes." In fact, I know many people who would have a difficult time describing a more peaceful or idyllic scene.

But what if you took that same little boat and placed it on the ocean—perhaps off the coast of the Pacific in my hometown of San Diego? Imagine yourself sitting in that boat as a storm rages overhead.

There's no gentle breeze now to tickle your skin, but instead a swirling tempest that stings your arms with rain. The waves lift your boat high into the air and then send it careening back down at roller-coaster speed. Water splashes over the sides of your vessel and soaks your clothes from tip to toe.

Would you feel at peace in that moment?

You probably have no desire to find out how you would respond to being stuck in a little boat during an ocean storm. Neither do I. But this exercise serves to remind us of an important point: most people define peace by looking at their external circumstances—at what's going on around them.

As Overcomers, however, we've been promised a peace that goes deeper—a peace that surpasses all understanding (Phil. 4:7) and allows us to cast all our anxieties on God (1 Pet. 5:7), no matter what circumstances we face.

PEACE IN THE STORM

Near the beginning of Jesus' public ministry, He and His disciples were sailing across the Sea of Galilee when they encountered a tempest of their own:

> Now when they had left the multitude, they took
> Him along in the boat as He was. And other little

boats were also with Him. And a great wind-storm arose, and the waves beat into the boat, so that it was already filling. But He was in the stern, asleep on a pillow. And they awoke Him and said to Him, "Teacher, do You not care that we are perishing?" (Mark 4:36–38)

For me, there is no greater image of peace that surpasses all understanding than this picture of Jesus—the ultimate Overcomer—sleeping on a pillow at the back of a boat while a storm raged around Him. That is the peace that comes from a confident, unwavering trust in God's plan. And that is the peace we have access to as Overcomers.

Of course, Jesus wasn't the only person in that boat. While Jesus slept, His disciples—many of them experienced fishermen—fought desperately against the storm. Their eyes were focused on their circumstances, which filled them with anxiety. When they finally turned their eyes to Jesus, they didn't take courage from His peace. Instead, they expressed consternation at His inaction: "do You not care that we are perishing?"

How many times have we asked some form of that question? *God, why don't You care? God, why haven't You fixed this? God, why am I still experiencing these trials and enduring this suffering?*

We ask those questions because we believe the lie that our lives are supposed to be smooth sailing on calm waters. The world tells us that our comfort and security should be our primary priorities—that they are basic human rights. Therefore, when a storm comes along to disrupt that comfort, we experience anxiety because we think we've been forgotten. Or betrayed. Or ignored. Or punished.

As Overcomers, the truth is that we've been created to function within the storms of life. We have a divine purpose and an eternal destiny that are anchored in the finished work of Jesus' death and resurrection. Therefore, we can walk confidently through any circumstance with the knowledge that we are secure in God's plan.

In other words, we can have peace because of what's inside us, rather than what is happening around us.

As Jesus' disciples discovered, that peace is ultimately based on His authority:

> Then He arose and rebuked the wind, and said to the sea, "Peace, be still!" And the wind ceased and there was a great calm. But He said to them, "Why are you so fearful? How is it that you have no faith?" And they feared exceedingly, and said to one another, "Who can this be, that even the wind and the sea obey Him!" (Mark 4:39–41)

The disciples were driven by anxiety because they did not understand who Jesus is, nor did they comprehend the value of His presence in their lives. But they eventually learned the truth, and so can we.

PEACE LEADS TO REJOICING

If your life isn't marked by an abundance of peace at the moment, that's okay. Jesus' disciples grew in their capacity to experience peace, and you can do the same.

Take Peter, for example. A little while after Jesus calmed the storm, Peter and the other disciples found themselves on another boat in the middle of another storm. This time, however, Jesus wasn't in the boat with them. He was walking on the waves. The disciples were initially terrified, thinking Jesus was a ghost. But when Jesus challenged them to reject their fear, Peter responded:

> And Peter answered Him and said, "Lord, if it is You, command me to come to You on the water."
>
> So He said, "Come." And when Peter had come down out of the boat, he walked on the water to go to Jesus. But when he saw that the wind was boisterous, he was afraid; and beginning to sink he cried out, saying, "Lord, save me!"
>
> And immediately Jesus stretched out His

hand and caught him, and said to him, "O you of little faith, why did you doubt?" And when they got into the boat, the wind ceased.

Then those who were in the boat came and worshiped Him, saying, "Truly You are the Son of God." (Matt. 14:28–33)

Do you see the evidence of growth? Yes, Peter still had his eyes on the circumstances around him, which caused anxiety. But he trusted Jesus enough to get out of the boat. And yes, Jesus asked the same question as in the previous storm: "Why did you doubt?" But this time the disciples didn't ask about His identity after He calmed the winds and the waves. This time they knew Him as "the Son of God."

Peter and the other disciples had grown in their knowledge of Jesus, which increased their capacity to trust Him—and their capacity to experience peace even during a storm.

Near the end of his life and having suffered incredible persecution in the name of Jesus, Peter wrote these words to the early church:

Dear friends, do not be surprised at the fiery ordeal that has come on you to test you, as though something strange were happening to you. But rejoice inasmuch as you participate in the sufferings of Christ, so that you may be overjoyed when his glory is revealed. (1 Peter 4:12–13, NIV)

What an amazing description of the peace we can experience as Overcomers. We know we will experience fiery ordeals throughout our lives— there's no reason to be surprised when trials arise and our safety and security are challenged. But instead of giving in to anxiety in those moments, we can trust in God's goodness and good purposes. We can trust in the security of our eternal destiny with our Savior in heaven.

Because of that trust, we can have peace. And not only peace, but we can rejoice even in the midst of suffering.

Heavenly Father,

I confess there are times when I take my eyes off You and look instead at the circumstances around me. Those circumstances can make me feel anxious. They can make me feel afraid.

Yet, I know You are increasing my capacity to trust in You. You are increasing my ability to experience peace even when things aren't going my way. And I accept those gifts from Your hand.

Thank You, Father, for the gift of peace. Amen.

CHAPTER 5

WE ARE PROMISED FAITH

George Mueller did not grow up as a man of faith. In fact, in his autobiography he described himself as a liar and a thief throughout his teenage years. Once Mueller accepted Jesus Christ as his Savior, however, everything changed. Mueller began to live as an Overcomer and literally changed the social fabric of nineteenth-century London through more than seven decades of ministry. His story endures today as an incredible testimony of the power of faith.

Here's how John Piper summarized Mueller's ministry:

He built five large orphan houses and cared for 10,024 orphans in his life. When he started in 1834 there were accommodations for 3,600 orphans in all of England and twice that many children under eight were in prison. One of the great effects of Mueller's ministry was to inspire others so that "fifty years after Mr. Mueller began his work, at least one hundred thousand orphans were cared for in England alone."

He did all this while he was preaching three times a week from 1830 to 1898, at least 10,000 times. And when he turned 70 he fulfilled a life-long dream of missionary work for the next 17 years until he was 87. He traveled to 42 countries, preaching on average of once a day, and addressing some three million people.[1]

What makes his story especially incredible is that George Mueller accomplished all of this without spending any time fundraising. Instead, when a need arose for any of the five orphanages—and needs arose on a daily basis—Mueller responded by praying.

As John Piper writes:

He had prayed in millions of dollars (in today's currency) for the Orphans and never asked anyone directly for money. He never took a salary in the last 68 years of his ministry, but trusted God to put in people's hearts to send him what he needed. He never took out a loan or went into debt. And neither he nor the orphans were ever hungry.[2]

George Mueller knew the power of actively demonstrating faith in God—the same power you and I have access to as Overcomers in God's kingdom.

THE TEST OF FAITH

Genesis 22 is one of the most shocking chapters in all of Scripture. It's also an incredible picture of God's love and care toward those who approach Him through faith.

Here's how it begins:

> Now it came to pass after these things that God tested Abraham, and said to him, "Abraham!"
>
> And he said, "Here I am."
>
> Then He said, "Take now your son, your only son Isaac, whom you love, and go to the land of Moriah, and offer him there as a burnt offering on one of the mountains of which I shall tell you."
> (vv. 1–2)

God's command was shocking for two reasons. First, while child sacrifice was common in the ancient world, God was (and is) staunchly opposed to that practice. He called it an "abomination" (Deut. 12:31) and declared that any parent who offered their child as a sacrifice must be put to death (Lev. 20:1–5).

Second, God's command was shocking because

Isaac himself was the result of a promise God had made to Abraham decades earlier. Abraham was seventy-five years old when God promised to bless him with a son and grow his descendants into "a great nation" (Gen. 12:1–3). And Abraham—along with his wife, Sarah—spent twenty-five years waiting in faith until Isaac was finally born (21:5).

Given these realities, can you imagine Abraham's frame of mind when God commanded him to sacrifice his son? Can you imagine the pain? Can you imagine what he must have been thinking as he "rose early" (22:3) the next morning and prepared for that terrible journey?

Actually, we don't have to imagine it. Because the Holy Spirit revealed what Abraham was thinking in the book of Hebrews:

> By faith Abraham, when he was tested, offered up Isaac, and he who had received the promises offered up his only begotten son, of whom it was said, "In Isaac your seed shall be called," *concluding that God was able to raise him up, even from the dead,* from which he also received him in a figurative sense. (11:17–19, emphasis added)

Abraham's faith in God was so strong that he believed God would raise Isaac from the dead rather than fail to keep His word.

THE REWARD OF FAITH

Of course, Genesis 22 has a happy ending. Having never intended any harm to Isaac, God provided a ram for Abraham to sacrifice in place of his son (v. 13). As a result, "Abraham called the name of the place, The-Lord-Will-Provide; as it is said to this day, 'In the Mount of the Lord it shall be provided'" (v. 14).

Moreover, Abraham's faith resulted in a reward not only for himself and his family but for all people:

> The angel of the Lord called to Abraham from heaven a second time and said, "I swear by myself, declares the Lord, that because you have done this and have not withheld your son, your only son, I will surely bless you and make your descendants as numerous as the stars in the sky and as the sand on the seashore. Your descendants will take possession of the cities of their enemies, and through your offspring all nations on earth will be blessed, because you have obeyed me." (vv. 15–18, NIV)

Don't miss the symbolism of that moment: in response to Abraham's faith, God spared the life of his son and provided a ram as a sacrifice in his place. Two thousand years later, God *did not* spare the life of His own Son, Jesus, who was offered once for all as a spotless Lamb in order that all people might receive forgiveness for their sins and be added to God's family.

That's the power of faith. And that's why faith must drive every moment of our lives as we seek to live out the message of the gospel in Jesus' name.

Heavenly Father,

I believe Your Word when it says without faith it is impossible to please You. And it is my sincere desire to please You. It's my desire to glorify You not only through who I am, but through everything I do.

Therefore, Father, please increase my faith. Increase my capacity to believe You—and to act on that belief. Thank You, Almighty God, for the gift of faith. Amen.

CHAPTER 6

WE ARE PROMISED WISDOM

As I write these words, there are more than 40,000 searches being conducted on Google every second. That's more than 3.5 billion searches per day, which is more than 1.2 trillion searches every year.[1]

Clearly, people today have a thirst for knowledge. But do we have a thirst for *wisdom*?

A recent study by the real estate blog *Estately* would suggest the answer is "No" a large portion of the time. The study used data from Google Trends to determine specific questions that were asked more often in a specific US state than in other states. Here are some of the results:

- People from California asked, "Where does bacon come from?" and, "Is a coconut a nut?"
- People from Indiana asked, "How many states are there?" and, "Is Bigfoot real?"
- People from Nevada wanted to know, "Who invented pizza?"

- And people from Texas asked, "Do zombies exist?"[2]

Now, as always, the world needs Overcomers who are filled not with more knowledge but with a deep thirst for God's wisdom.

THE SOURCE OF WISDOM

One question people should be asking in today's world is this: "Where can I find wisdom?" And as with every important question, the answer is found within the pages of God's Word:

> If any of you lacks wisdom, let him ask of God, who gives to all liberally and without reproach, and it will be given to him. But let him ask in faith, with no doubting, for he who doubts is like a wave of the sea driven and tossed by the wind. (James 1:5–6)

There are two things to keep in mind as we engage these verses.

First, wisdom is free for the taking. Or, to be more accurate, wisdom is free for the asking.

There are no complicated formulas we need to process in order to increase the amount of wisdom in our lives. There are no hoops we need to jump through—no amount of points we need to score or credits we need to earn. We need only ask our Father, and He will give us wisdom.

And notice, He won't give us the bare minimum amount of wisdom. He won't give us just enough to get by. No, our heavenly Father "gives to all liberally and without reproach." He will fill our cups to overflowing with divine wisdom—if we will only take the time to earnestly seek Him and ask for what we need.

Second, when we ask God for wisdom, we need to let go of our doubts. We need to ask Him "in faith, with no doubting."

What this means on a practical level is that we need to ask God with the expectation of receiving an answer. Faith is revealed not just by believing something but by doing something. Faith is belief in action.

Therefore, if we ask God for wisdom to make a decision or choose a path through life, we must be ready to act when our request is answered and we receive the wisdom we need. Otherwise we will be like a wave tossed back and forth by the wind— always at the mercy of our circumstances.

THE CHARACTER OF WISDOM

Our heavenly Father is the source of wisdom. But what is wisdom, and how will we recognize it when we receive it? Once again, we can find answers in the book of James.

First, James offers a detailed look at what wisdom *is not*:

> Who is wise and understanding among you? Let him show by good conduct that his works are done in the meekness of wisdom. But if you have bitter envy and self-seeking in your hearts, do not boast and lie against the truth. This wisdom does not descend from above, but is earthly, sensual, demonic. For where envy and self-seeking exist, confusion and every evil thing are there. (James 3:13–16)

If you are seeking wisdom on a certain issue, and you receive an answer that lines up exactly with everything you want—be cautious. Godly wisdom is not self-seeking. We must always be on guard against seeking our own plans and our own goals rather than seeking God's will.

Likewise, if you feel led in a direction that allows you to indulge in sensual pleasures or goes against the principles established in God's Word, that's not wisdom. Nor is it wisdom for us to walk down a path that leads to boastfulness or pride. The wisdom of the world is a far cry from God's wisdom.

Thankfully, James gave us a clear picture of what God's wisdom looks like in our daily lives:

> But the wisdom that is from above is first pure, then peaceable, gentle, willing to yield, full of mercy and good fruits, without partiality and without hypocrisy. Now the fruit of righteousness is sown in peace by those who make peace. (James 3:17–18)

Godly wisdom leads to godliness. It creates peace in our lives and in the lives of those around us—not confusion. It helps us obey Jesus by placing others ahead of ourselves. It drives us to be impartial rather than selfish or self-centered.

In short, when we receive wisdom from Christ, we will behave more like Christ. And we will be transformed more and more into His image. That is the gift we've been given as Overcomers—the wisdom of God.

Will you receive it?

Heavenly Father,

In obedience to Your Word, I ask for wisdom so that I can make decisions that align with Your will. I ask for wisdom so that I can see the path You have laid out for me.

I ask in faith, Father, believing that You give

generously and without reproach. I ask as Your serv-ant who is prepared to take action based on what I am about to receive.

Lord God, thank You for the gift of wisdom. Amen.

CHAPTER 7

WE ARE PROMISED VICTORY OVER TEMPTATION

When C. S. Lewis published *Mere Christianity* in 1952, people all over the world recognized it to be a thoughtful and practical guide to the Christian life, and people all over the world believe the same today. The book has aged well.

Still, sometimes it can be surprising how well Lewis's descriptions apply to modern life. For example, I was recently struck by his profound warnings about temptation, including the following:

A silly idea is current that good people do not know what temptation means. This is an obvious lie. Only those who try to resist temptation know how strong it is. After all, you find out the strength of the German army by fighting against it, not by giving in. You find out the strength of a wind by trying to walk against it, not by lying down. A man who gives in to temptation after five minutes simply does not know what it would have been like an hour later.[1]

Today, as in Lewis's time, there is a false perception within the church (and within our culture) that healthy Christians do not struggle with the reality of sin in their lives. Many people believe that mature Christians "have it all together"—that they have reached a certain level of spiritual perfection in which they don't even experience temptation.

Let me put that myth to rest. All Christians are pushed and tempted toward sinful behavior because all Christians exist in a world corrupted by sin. What is more, we have an enemy who desires nothing greater than to see faithful members of God's kingdom dragged down by moral failures of one kind or another.

You don't need me to tell you that temptation exists all around us. You have experienced it for yourself, and you will continue to experience it even as you mature as an Overcomer. Still, neither you nor I should concede defeat. Far from it! As Overcomers, we have been promised victory over temptation.

YOU ARE FREED FROM SIN

I believe sin has never been as accessible as it is now, and evil has never been so user-friendly. Our technologies, mixed with the sinful tendencies of our fallen nature and intensified by Satan, have put a capital *T* in Temptation. And our loss of a clear North Star of morality and self-control has only made it worse.

That's the bad news. The good news is that, as Overcomers in God's kingdom, we have the legal and spiritual authority to reject temptation and choose the righteousness of Christ.

The apostle Paul wrote about that authority in his epistle to the church in Rome:

> For if we have been united together in the likeness of His death, certainly we also shall be in the likeness of His resurrection, knowing this, that our old man was crucified with Him, that the body of sin might be done away with, that we should no longer be slaves of sin. For he who has died has been freed from sin. (Romans 6:5–7)

Do you realize that before your salvation, you were a slave to sin? Your body and mind were under the rule of a cruel master, and your very instincts were corrupted. Your decisions were sinful because you were full of sin.

But now, having experienced the forgiveness of sin through faith in the death and resurrection of Jesus Christ, you are a slave to sin no longer. You are free. As Paul wrote in another epistle: "Therefore, if anyone is in Christ, he is a new creation; old things have passed away; behold, all things have become new" (2 Corinthians 5:17).

And there's more: the fact that you were "crucified with" Jesus means you have legally been separated from the power of sin. Death is the great breaker of contracts, and by participating in the death and resurrection of Jesus, sin no longer has any legal authority in your life.

As Paul wrote: "For the death that [Jesus] died, He died to sin once for all; but the life that He lives, He lives to God. Likewise you also, reckon yourselves to be dead indeed to sin, but alive to God in Christ Jesus our Lord" (Romans 6:10–11).

YOU CAN SAY "NO" TO SIN

The result of our legal separation from sin is that we can legally say "No" to temptation. We don't have to be defeated by temptation. We don't have to be enslaved by lust or gluttony or greed or selfishness or pride or any other instrument of temptation. We have been granted victory over sin, which means we can simply reject its power and say "Yes" to Christ's continued work in our lives.

Look at Paul's continued instructions in Romans 6:

41

- "Therefore do not let sin reign in your mortal body, that you should obey it in its lusts. And do not present your members as instruments of unrighteousness to sin, but present yourselves to God as being alive from the dead, and your members as instruments of righteousness to God" (vv. 12–13).

- "Do you not know that to whom you present yourselves slaves to obey, you are that one's slaves whom you obey, whether of sin leading to death, or of obedience leading to righteousness?" (v. 16).

- "I speak in human terms because of the weakness of your flesh. For just as you presented your members as slaves of uncleanness, and of lawlessness leading to more lawlessness, so now present your members as slaves of righteousness for holiness" (v. 19).

Do you see the emphasis on who takes the action in these verses? We do! We can say "No" to sin. We have that power—and that responsibility.

I have known many Christians who believed they were still especially susceptible to specific types of sin. "I'm just a lustful person," they say. Or, "I have a natural bent toward laziness, but I'm working on it." What these people mean when they say these things is that sin is still part of who they are. That there are some impulses they still cannot control.

This is a false belief. The truth is that sin is not part of who we *are*—it's part of who we *were* before we encountered Christ. Before we were made new. That doesn't mean we will be perfect from this point forward, but we can be better. We can be victorious over sin.

We can be Overcomers.

Heavenly Father,

I proclaim my belief in the death and resurrection of Jesus Christ, and I declare the forgiveness of my sin through His blood that was shed on the cross. I am no longer a slave to sin. I am free.

Because of that freedom, I will say "No" to sin. I will not allow sin to reign in my mortal body. Instead, I will choose to walk in the victory You have provided for me.

Thank You, Father, for victory over temptation. Amen.

CHAPTER 8

WE ARE PROMISED ANSWERS TO OUR PRAYERS

Since the early 1980s, scientists and volunteers from around the world have been involved in the SETI project—the Search for Extra-Terrestrial Intelligence. The goal of this project is to constantly scan the cosmos in search of any sign of alien life.

As you might imagine, the SETI project is inherently passive. It's a waiting game.

Things changed in 2017, however, with the launch of the METI project—as in Messaging Extra-Terrestrial Intelligence. That's when scientists beamed a message directly toward a planetary system orbiting GJ 273, otherwise known as Luyten's Star. That system contains a potentially habitable planet, which means there could possibly be sentient beings there to hear the message—and respond. The message was repeated over three separate days so that anyone listening would know it wasn't an accident. It contained basic formulas from math and physics, along with brief excerpts of music recordings.

Unfortunately, scientists with the METI project won't be hearing a response anytime soon. Because Luyten's Star is twelve lightyears away, it will take a minimum of twelve years for the message to reach that system—and twelve more years for any reply to reach us. That means the earliest the METI project could hear a response would be 2042.

And the chances of receiving that response are slim. "Practically speaking, if we get a signal from Luyten's Star, it will mean the Milky Way is teeming with life. It's certainly possible," said Doug Vakoch, the president and founder of METI. "It seems more likely that we'll need to target not just one star, but hundreds, thousands, or even millions before we get a reply back."[1]

As Overcomers, we don't have to settle for opening the lines of communication with a single planet, or even a single galaxy, wondering if anyone is listening. We have direct access to the Creator of the universe through prayer. And we have the confidence of knowing He will respond.

GOD HEARS OUR PRAYERS

As I've talked with people about prayer throughout my ministry, there's a question that seems to come up over and over again: "How can I be sure God hears me when I pray?" I've often heard people express frustration with the practice of prayer because they aren't sure if they are doing it correctly, or they feel as if their prayers are bouncing off the roof instead of rising into God's presence.

If you've ever felt a similar frustration with the practice of prayer, take heart in the fact that you're not alone. I've experienced those frustrations as well. I've had seasons where it seems as if the words I speak to God are filled with lead and clunk down to the floor as soon as they leave my mouth.

As Overcomers, we need to understand two truths about prayer—and the first is that our enemy knows the power of prayer. Satan does not want you to pray, and he especially does not want you to develop the discipline of a prayer-filled life. Therefore, he will speak discouragement into your heart and mind around the practice of prayer. He will seek to convince you that God doesn't have time to deal with the trivial matters of your life, or that you are not worthy of approaching God's throne in prayer, or that God simply doesn't care.

That leads me to the second truth we need to understand about prayer: God hears our prayers. All of them. Every single one. How do I know? Because that truth has been made clear in His Word:

- "This is the confidence we have in approaching God: that if we ask anything according to his will, he hears us. And if we know that he hears us—whatever we ask—we know that we have what we asked of him" (1 John 5:14–15, NIV).

- "O Lord, You have searched me and known me. . . . For there is not a word on my tongue, but behold, O Lord, You know it altogether" (Ps. 139:1,4).

- "Let us therefore come boldly to the throne of grace, that we may obtain mercy and find grace to help in time of need" (Heb. 4:16).

As an Overcomer in God's kingdom, you have direct access to God's throne through prayer. Never forget that truth. Never ignore it. Never underestimate its importance in your life.

GOD ANSWERS OUR PRAYERS

Not only do we have a promise that God hears our prayers, but we can have confidence that God will answer our prayers as well. Every single one.

The apostle Paul knew the value of prayer. Therefore, when he was confronted with a situation that felt intolerable—likely a physical ailment such as trouble with his eyesight—he turned to God in prayer to ask for help:

> And lest I should be exalted above measure by the abundance of the revelations, a thorn in the flesh was given to me, a messenger of Satan to buffet me, lest I be exalted above measure. Concerning this thing I pleaded with the Lord three times that it might depart from me. And He said to me, "My grace is sufficient for you, for My strength is made perfect in weakness." (2 Cor. 12:7–9)

Paul felt strongly enough about this "thorn in the flesh" to make three separate appeals for God to remove it. And in each case, God answered Paul's prayer by saying "No."

That's something we need to remember as we make our requests known to God: "No" is an answer. We may not understand it, and we may not like it—but there will be times when God denies our requests. There will also be times when God says "Wait." And there will certainly be times when God chooses to answer "Yes."

As Overcomers, we have the privilege of seeking God through prayer. Yet we also carry the responsibility of submitting to God's answers—even if those answers don't align with our desires.

Still, look what happened when God said "No" to Paul's request to remove his thorn in the flesh: "Therefore most gladly I will rather boast in my infirmities, that the power of Christ may rest upon me. Therefore I take pleasure in infirmities, in reproaches, in needs, in persecutions, in distresses, for Christ's sake. For when I am weak, then I am strong" (2 Cor. 12:9–10).

Do you see the miracle in these verses? God allowed the thorn to remain so that Paul could experience "the power of Christ"—and even "take pleasure" in his difficult circumstances. Paul wanted relief from pain, but God had a better plan. God granted Paul the grace and the strength to glorify Him even in the midst of his pain.

Will you commit to the practice of prayer? If so, you can have confidence that your prayers will be heard and answered in a way that will strengthen you to live as an Overcomer.

Heavenly Father,

I believe Your Word is true; therefore, I know You hear my prayers. I can come before Your throne not because I am worthy but because I am wrapped in the righteousness of Jesus Christ.

Father, I know You will not only hear my prayers but answer them. You will provide what I need, and

You will show me Your will. I accept it. I submit to Your answers and to Your will even as I continue to pray.

Thank You, Father, for the gift of answered prayers. Amen.

NOTES

INTRODUCTION

1. "Messages from General Dwight D. Eisenhower Prior and After Normandy D-Day," American Merchant Marine at War, accessed June 20, 2018, http://www.usmm.org /ikedday.html.

2. Scott Simon, "The Speech Eisenhower Never Gave on the Normandy Invasion," NPR (06/08/2013), https://www.npr.org/2013/06/08/189535104/the-speech-eisenhower-never-gave-on-the-normandy-invasion.

CHAPTER 1: WE ARE PROMISED STRENGTH

1. "Ray Williams Hits First-Ever 1,000 Pound Raw (No Wraps) Squat in Powerlifting History," Barbend (10/16/2016), https://barbend.com/ray-williams-1000-pound-squat-history/.

CHAPTER 2: WE ARE PROMISED TRUTH

1. "'Fake News' Is 2017 American Dialect Society Word of the Year," American Dialect Society (01/05/2018), https://www.americandialect.org/fake-news-is-2017-american-dialect-society-word-of-the-year.

2. A. W. Tozer, "Truth Is a Person," the Alliance (08/02/2015), https://www.cmalliance .org/devotions/tozer?id=160.

CHAPTER 3: WE ARE PROMISED GOODNESS

1. Frederick Buechner, *Secrets in the Dark: A Life in Sermons* (New York, NY: HarperCollins Publishers, 2006), 128.

CHAPTER 5: WE ARE PROMISED FAITH

1. John Piper, "George Mueller's Strategy for Showing God," Desiring God (02/03/2004), https://www.desiringgod.org/messages/george-muellers-strategy-for-showing-god.

2. Ibid.

CHAPTER 6: WE ARE PROMISED WISDOM

1. "Google Search Statistics," Internet Live Stats, accessed July 7, 2018, http://www.internet livestats.com/google-search-statistics/.

2. Ryan Nickum, "You Won't Believe the Questions Each State Googles More Than Any Other State," Estately (05/24/2016), https://www.estately.com/blog/2016/05/you-wont -believe-the-questions-each-state-googles-more-than-any-other-state/.

CHAPTER 7: WE ARE PROMISED VICTORY OVER TEMPTATION

1. C. S. Lewis, *Mere Christianity* (San Francisco: Harper San Francisco, 2001), 142.

CHAPTER 8: WE ARE PROMISED ANSWERS TO OUR PRAYERS

1. Eric Mack, "We Just Sent a Message to Aliens Who Could Respond by 2042," CNET (11/16/2017), https://www.cnet.com/news/seti-space-aliens-extra-terrestrial -intelligence-luytens-star-gj-273/.

TAKE THE NEXT STEP!

You've seen the promises. Are you ready
to take a deeper look at what it means
to live each day as an Overcomer?

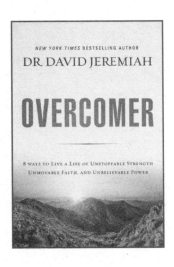

In *Overcomer*, bestselling author Dr. David
Jeremiah uses Paul's instructions in Ephesians 6—
his command for us to overcome the forces of evil
by putting on the armor of God—to lay out a pathway
for spiritual victory. Dr. Jeremiah also reminds us
that we're not alone in this fight. God knows what we
need, and He provides us with His power so we can
face life's challenges poised for success.